LOOKING TO THE HEAVEN WITHIN
ಹೊಂ
LOOKING TO THE HELL WITHOUT

Poems of Contemplation
Volume Four

Alexander R. DeSantiago

© Copyright 2004 Alexander R. DeSantiago.
All rights reserved. No part of this publication may be reproduced, stored in a retrieval system, or transmitted, in any form or by any means, electronic, mechanical, photocopying, recording, or otherwise, without the written prior permission of the author.

Note for Librarians: a cataloguing record for this book that includes Dewey Decimal Classification and US Library of Congress numbers is available from the Library and Archives of Canada. The complete cataloguing record can be obtained from their online database at:
www.collectionscanada.ca/amicus/index-e.html
ISBN 1-4120-4466-9

TRAFFORD

Offices in Canada, USA, Ireland, UK and Spain
This book was published *on-demand* in cooperation with Trafford Publishing. On-demand publishing is a unique process and service of making a book available for retail sale to the public taking advantage of on-demand manufacturing and Internet marketing. On-demand publishing includes promotions, retail sales, manufacturing, order fulfilment, accounting and collecting royalties on behalf of the author.

Book sales for North America and international:
Trafford Publishing, 6E–2333 Government St.,
Victoria, BC v8t 4p4 CANADA
phone 250 383 6864 (toll-free 1 888 232 4444)
fax 250 383 6804; email to orders@trafford.com

Book sales in Europe:
Trafford Publishing (uk) Ltd., Enterprise House, Wistaston Road Business Centre, Wistaston Road, Crewe, Cheshire cw2 7rp UNITED KINGDOM
phone 01270 251 396 (local rate 0845 230 9601)
facsimile 01270 254 983; orders.uk@trafford.com

Order online at:
www.trafford.com/robots/04-2274.html

10 9 8 7 6 5 4 3 2

THIS VOLUME
IS DEDICATED
TO MY WIFE ALICIA
AND OUR DAUGHTER ARIELLE
FOR THE HAPPINESS THEY BRING TO ME
IS TRULY
A GIFT FROM GOD

INTRODUCTION

As the title states, the poems contained in this volume are of a contemplative nature. They are intended to be a study of life itself, the world in which we live, and the things we consider right or wrong. They are also intended to question the reader, bring that same reader to question oneself, and wonder whether the environments we reside in are truly the way things should be. So, as you become familiar with the text, consider what it is you believe to be just or unjust, proper or improper, selfish or unselfish. Then, ask yourself if these ideas you believe are a product of that which you have learned by your own choice, or merely what you have been told to think. Also, these same poems of which I write are not intended to be abstract, difficult to understand, or pretentious in language and feel. For, I believe poetry should be simple, it should challenge the status quo, and realize the injustices of the world. Therefore, I will feel no need to appear as an intellectual, but only as an equal to any and all of my brothers and sisters. After all, one can only hope that in the end, a simple fact such as this, will become the only truth we care to know.

Alexander R. DeSantiago
September, 2004

FOREWARD

    The poetry printed herein, with the exception of four last minute additions, was written within the months of February, March, April, and May of 2004. The titles I chose to add before publication are as follows: COLORED JESUS, FREEDOM IS, FAIL SAFE, and KEY. These were written through the end of July, and the beginning of August of the same year. The subject matter was taken from everyday life, expanded through the study of the human condition, the world we have created, and the questions that give rise to such study. The format in which they are presented will come in two parts with four sections each. Overall, the first section shows my religious background, and will offer a ray of hope in the beginning. But, as with everything else, succeeding sections will testify to the contradictions we face, the hollow promises that stem from such contradictions and the loss of hope that grows from these. There will be small instances, throughout the text, where a minute point of faith in the human race will be offered, but they will be few and far between. As is the life we live. Coming to the finish of this book, as you eventually will, I ask you to consider one last thing. Do we choose to give the story of the human race, a sad ending or not?

    Alexander R. DeSantiago
    September, 2004

CONTENTS

PART ONE
LOOKING TO THE HEAVEN WITHIN

SECTION ONE
DO WE

Do We	5
Serenity's Garden	6
Be Not Afraid	7
Around The Cross	8
Permit	9
Foretold	10
As You Will	11
Light And Love	12
Appearance	13
By And By	14
Tick Tock	15
Easter	16
Unworthy Love	17
My Friend	18
Life!	19
Mr. Rogers' World	20
Tolerance	21
Listen	22
Let Me Be	23
Man From Ghana	24
Theologian	26
Verga	27
How Then	28
Closer	29
Neighbor	30
Colored Jesus	31

SECTION TWO
HIM

Learn To Lose 35
A Father's Anxiety 36
Crazed 37
Draft 38
Blue 39
Unprepared 40
If He 41
Overexposed 42
Don't Care 43
Freedom Fleet 44
Fed Up 45
Artful Deception 46
Apparently Not 47

SECTION THREE
FAMILY

Rehearsal For Strings 51
Shadow 52
Knowing That 53
Identity's Death 54

SECTION FOUR
AMERICA

Fear In San Francisco 59
Jazz Renaissance 60
Plea 62
Mourning Patrol 64
Columbine 66
Is This Our Flag? 67
Book Store 68
Freedom's Law 69
Gay Marriage 70

War On Terror 71
Amended 72
Might Makes Fright 73
We Want You 74
911 76
Falling Sky 78
Make Over 79
All You Know 80
Altamont Past 81
Fair Share 82
Scapegoat 84
Yesterday, Today, Tomorrow 86
Fail Safe 87
Freedom Is 90
Naivete' 92
Near End 93
Indeed 94

PART TWO
LOOKING TO
THE HELL WITHOUT

SECTION FIVE
DO WE NOT

Do We Not 101
I Know God! 102
Evil 103
Little Love 104
Shunned 105
Lost Love 106
Stream 107
Freeway 108
Abyss 109

Preference 110
Rhyme Devoid 111
Insane Hope 112
Life As A Violin 113
Mortality 114

SECTION SIX
FATHERS AND SONS

Grounder 117
Unknown Fear 118
His Is His 119
Fathers And Sons 120
Michael 122
Guilt 123

SECTION SEVEN
HUMAN

Awakened Lie 127
Theatre 128
Irony 132
Fault Line 133
Do You See? 134
Two Parts Being 135
Eccentric 136
So Much Nonsense 137
Surrounded 138
Point 139
Mouth 140
Violenceus Domesticus 141
Sensibilities 142
Opinion 143
Pretension 144
Abuse 145
Childhood 146

Hunt 147
Void Of Distinction 148
Kind Of Blind 149
Key 150

SECTION EIGHT
WORLD

Two Faces 153
Graffitti 154
Abortion 155
Feel 156
Fly 157
One Owner 158
Wasteland 159
Sap 160
Beyond 161
Roar 162
Truth Be Told 163
Tabula Rasa 164
Meadow 165
Ocean 166
Rabbit 167
Regressive Dialogue 168
Affluent Pollutant 169
Progress 170
Schism 171
Pollution 172
Earth Day 173
Musical Showcase 174
Acknowledgements 175

PART ONE

LOOKING TO
THE HEAVEN WITHIN

SECTION ONE

DO WE

Do We

Do We

See Our Own Silence

With Providence

Do We

Observe Our Own Stillness

With Prowess

Do We

Witness Our Own Serenity

With Proximity

Looking To The Heaven Within

Serenity's Garden

In My Garden

Of Serenity

Exists A Calmly Felt Security

In My Garden

Of Serenity

Dwells A Richly Diverse Society

In My Garden

Of Serenity

Comes A Solemnly Understood Piety

In My Garden

Of Serenity

Lives A Beauty For All Eternity

Be Not Afraid

Be Not Afraid
Of What You Are

Be Not Afraid
Of Him

Be Not Afraid
Of A Terrible Scar
To Be Called
Original Sin

Be Not Afraid
To Open Your Heart

Be Not Afraid
To Love

Be Not Afraid
To Become A Part
Of His Call
For All From Above

Around The Cross

Around The Cross

Appeared Not

Money

Nor Stature

Wealth Nor Grandeur

Around The Cross

Appeared

Humility

And Tenderness

Love And Forgiveness

Around The Cross

Appeared Not

But

GOD's Children

Permit

Forgive And Forget
Love Not Regret

Absolve And Omit
Know Not Resent

Pardon And Permit
A Chance To Repent

Foretold

A Mirror Foretold
A Deceiver Of Old

A Mirror Foretold
A Sinner So Bold

A Mirror Foretold
A Believer Though Cold
Can Be Warmed
In Heart And Soul
Made Whole
Through Love
A Grace Given
By Our Risen
LORD

As You Will

LORD

Do With Me As You Will

STILL

My Anguished Heart

LORD

Make Of Me As You See Fit

KNIT

My Loosened Strands Of Life

LORD

Mold Of Me As You Would Do

TOO

My Misshapen Past

LORD

Speak To Me As You Would Say

PRAY

My Soul's Desire Climbing Ever Higher

EVER NEARER TO YOU

Light And Love

FATHER

IN HEAVEN

YOU ARE

THE LIGHT IN MY SOUL

YOU ARE

THE LOVE IN THE WHOLE

OF MY BEING

Appearance

LORD

As Such

I May Not Appear

As Much

To The Eye

Of My

Human Family

But

IN YOU I TRUST

As Much

That I May Appear

As Such

To Be

What You See In Me

As Worthy Of Your Love

By And By

Raise Jesus

Up On A Pedestal

Raise Jesus

Up On High

Where From His Will

We All Can Fly

On Up To Heaven

By And By

Tick Tock

TICK

TOCK

TICK

TOCK

YOUR TIME WILL COME
BETTER BE READY
WHEN THE SUM
OF ALL YOU HAVE DONE
IS JUDGED
TO BE
PURELY FORGIVEN

Easter

On Easter Sundays
Are Family Fun Days
Where Love And Forgiveness
Are Witnessed

On Easter Sundays
Are Family Run Days
Where Eggshells Of Heaven
Are Hidden

On Easter Sundays
Are Family One Days
Where Souls Can Be Found
Raised From The Ground
To Abound
With A Sound
Of Peace

Unworthy Love

I Am Not Worthy

Though I Receive

I Am Not Upright

Though I Follow

I Am Not Righteous

Though I Listen

I Am Not Holy

Though I Accept

My LORD Loves Me

My Friend

My Friend Jesus
Comes A Calling When
Ever My Heart
Hangs Low

My Friend Jesus
Comes A Calling When
Ever My Love
Comes Slow

My Friend Jesus
Comes A Calling When
Ever My Hate
Grows Bold

My Friend Jesus
Comes A Calling When
Ever My Day
Turns Cold

My Friend Jesus
Comes A Calling When
Ever My Life
Fills With Sorrow

My Friend Jesus
Comes A Calling When
Ever My Soul
Is An Empty Hole

Life!

The Sun
Took A Vacation Today.

A Very Good Idea
I Must Say.

Though I Missed Him
It Was Well Deserved.

For Within Him
Comes A Holy Word.

LIFE!

Mr. Rogers' World

The World

According To Mr. Rogers

Is Beautiful Indeed

A Freed Sense Of Wonder

For Those In Need

Of His Wisdom

In Loving Spirit

Of His Comfort

In Words We Could Hear It

The Seed

We Should Heed

To Grow

With Speed

To Shade

The Weed

And Become

The Ultimate Destination

Of Peace

Tolerance

I Know
A Good Word
It Begins With A "T"

It Speaks To Me
Of A "PEACE"
That Could Be

If Only We
Would Understand
The True Meaning Of "FREE"

In This Land
Of "LIBERTY"
Where "TOLERANCE" For Thee

My "BROTHER"
Can See
How He Can "LOVE" Unconditionally

Listen

Listen To My Story
Of A Once Upon A Time
When Apathy's Crime
Stood Alone
Never Known

Listen To My Tale
Of A Once Upon A Day
When Hatred's Ray
Flew Alone
Never Shown

Listen To My Fable
Of A Once Upon A Past
When Anger At Last
Died Alone
Never Sown

Let Me Be

Let Me Be
Less Than I Am

Let Me See
How I Can Stand

Myself Without Anger
My Heart Without Hate
My Mind Without Malice
My Soul Without Evil

Man From Ghana

The Man From Ghana
Smiled
Even As He Spoke
Of Starvation He Knew As A Child

The Man From Ghana
Joked
Even As He Talked
Of His Poverty's Heavy Yoke

The Man From Ghana
Grinned
Even As He Stood
As An Example To The Wind Of Oppression
With An Expression Of Happiness
In Thanks For His Blessings
WE HAVE

So Long Taken For Granted
The Man From Ghana
Impressed Me
For He

Knew The True

The Real

The View We Fail To See

That We Prove To Be

Blind To How Lucky

WE ARE

Complacent By Far

And Few Between Have Seen

THAT

To Give

Our Comfort To The Needy

Our Contentment To The Poor

Is To Live

In Quiet Harmony

In Peace And Love

Theologian

ALLEGEDLY

SUPPOSEDLY

POSSIBLY

COULD BE

MAYBE

UNLIKELY

YET WE

CONTINUE TOO

BELIEVE THROUGH

OUR FATHER'S HEAVENLY GRACE

Verga

Picture

Of Pestilence

Passover Way

Back In Time

Must Have Appeared

Similar To This

Hiss Of Fate

This Hardened Heart Hate

Within Pharaoh Where

Flew The Arrow There

Of Mighty High

Personal Lie

To Die

By

The Hand Of GOD

How Then

I Want.
Yet, I Should Not.
But, If I Should Not.
Then, How Should I Not
Attain Heaven?

I Deserve.
Yet, I Do Not.
But, If I Do Not.
Then, How Do I Not
Attain Paradise?

I Need
Yet, I Will Not.
But, If I Will Not.
Then, How Will I Not
Attain Life?

Closer

Closer

I Come To My GOD

Yet

More Sadness I Feel

For

I Begin To Understand

My

Pain Has Yet To Heal

Neighbor

Love Thy Neighbor
ACCEPT WHEN
Convicted Of Molestation

Love Thy Neighbor
ACCEPT WHEN
Proven A Sneak Thief

Love Thy Neighbor
ACCEPT WHEN
Prosecuted For Assassination

Love Thy Neighbor
ACCEPT WHEN
Filled With Sorrow's Grief
Upon Our Time
Upon Our Rhyme
And Rhythm Life
Broken By
A Token Lie

Colored Jesus

What Color
Would Jesus Be
If He Appeared Suddenly?

Would His Skin Be Dark?

Would It Be Light?

What Do You Think
Would Be Right
To Assume Beneath White
Robed Splendor?

Could He Be Blue?

Or, Maybe Green?

It Doesn't Seem
Possible. Though

It Can Appear
Probable, No?

To Believe
We Could Deceive Ourselves

Into Thinking
We Should Expect Anything Good.

To Come
From All We Perceive

As Known
To Be True In Our Point Of View.

Tell Me.
Do You

Think He Would Have
Any Color At All?

SECTION TWO

HIM

Learn To Lose

The More He Learns
Of The Human Race
The More He Loses
Of Hope

The More He Uncovers
Of The Human Face
The More He Misplaces
Of Trust

The More He Hears
Of The Human Case
The More He Forfeits
Of Faith

The More He Discovers
Of The Human Base
The More He Gives
Of Love

A Father's Anxiety

He Must Protect His Family

From A Wreck Of Insanity

Drawing Upon The Mind

Of Future Human Kind

Exploding Outward

Creeping Inward

Infecting Sense

Taut And Tense

Intelligence

Crazed

A Laughter

Half Crazed

Wholly Amazed

At A Waste Of Human Life

Given As A Gift Extraordinaire

Comes To Tear Away The Veil

Of Understanding Timeless Patience

Is Kneaded And Beaten

Is Poured And Formed

Into A Mold Of Wanting

Baked And Sold On A Rack Of Wishing

To Be

Finally

Something Worthy

Of Human Fancy

Draft

Sadness Pervades
Most Of His Work
Seeking To Usurp
His Chance To Be
Truly Happy

Sadness Penetrates
Most Of His Toil
Seeking To Spoil
His Turn To Be
Truly Care Free

Sadness Permeates
Most Of His Craft
Seeking To Draft
His Fate To Be
Truly Unlucky

Blue

Mr. Blue

How Are You?

It's Been A Short Time

Since Last We Met.

I Bet

We're Getting On In Years

Living With Fears

Drenched In Tears.

Mr. Blue

How Have You Been?

We've Known A Long Time

Since First We Met.

To Let

This Feeling Run It's Course

From The Source

Of Old Remorse.

Mr. Blue

It's Been Nice To See You?

Yet, Once Again Comes A Time

Now That We've Met.

To Set

Your Emotion Aside

Where It Can Hide

Deep Inside.

Until

The Tide

Turns Back

Once More To Restore

Your Color As Before.

Unprepared

Framed Family Pictures

Prepared For Show

Prearranged To Glow

Remain Hidden Below

Tucked Away

You Know

For

To Bring Himself To Hang Them

Must Acknowledge A Sin

Too Difficult To Bare

Witness To A Tear

Upon A Garment Of Pain

Full Of Past Memory Never Mended

If He

IF

It Weren't For His Wife

HE

Would Hate His Life

IF

It Weren't For His Daughter

HE

Would Give Forth No Laughter

IF

It Weren't For His Son

HE

Would Know Nothing Of Fun

IF

It Weren't For His Family

HE

Would So Steadily

DROWN IN A SEA OF DEPRESSION

Overexposed

Oh, Lost Youth

Lost Hope If Only

He Could Reclaim

All Which He Has Longed For

All Which He Has Needed

Within The Darkness

Of His Painful Past

At Last To Understand

What IT Was

He Missed

When Searching Through Eyes

Blurred By Tears Of Wondering

Why

Must The Lie

Remain

Unexposed

To Those

Who Could Help

A Hated Whelp

Don't Care

He Doesn't Care

Anymore

To Stare

Within A Mirror

To Fear

Himself

Of Truth

Of Hated Youth

Drenched And Drowning

In Tears Of A Pounding

Heartless One

Is He

Thee?

Freedom Fleet

His Car Died

TODAY

And

He Wished

He'd Killed It Himself

To Set Upon A Shelf

Those Momentary Freedoms

Bringing Stinging Realizations

Someday

Somehow

He Should Learn

NOW

It Is Time

To Reject

The Infection

That Is

Man's Every New Invention

Fed Up

Twisted Ankle

Twice A Week

Sometimes Three

Of Thee Falling

To A Bruising

Ego's Anger

Burning Hot

Stretching Not

Enough To Gratify

Nor, Ever Satisfy

Fated Humor

Laughing At Thee

Of Injury

Again And Again

What Is Thy Sin?

Thou Should Suffer

So Within

Muscular

Atrophied

Stature

Artful Deception

He Had A Dream
Last Night

A Beautiful
Wonderful Dream

Where The Seam
Of Lie

Was Torn Apart
With The Face Of Art

Full Of Deception
Upon A Man

Who Would Dare Stand

To Be An Example
Of Adulthood

He Had A Dream
Last Night

A Horrible
Hateful Dream

Where It Seemed
He Cried

As He Tore Apart
The Face Of Art

Full With Deception
Upon A Man

Who Could Not Stand

To Be An Example
Of Life

Apparently Not

Apparently

He Was Wrong

To Believe

In Any Sort Of Song

Of Reprieve

From Along

Tortured Existence

Apparently

He Was Mistaken

To Hold

With Any Sort Of Suspension

Of A Cold

Form Of Continuation

In Tormented Essence

SECTION THREE

FAMILY

Rehearsal For Strings

He Sees
Her Play Today And

He Feels
As An Older Man Does When

He Kneels
At The Foot Of Memory

Where She
Exists In Baby Steps Of Beginning

Of Growing To Be Impressive To See
How Far Has She Come To Thee

BEAUTY

All Encompassed

Shadow

DOG!

What Do You Think

You Are

A Frog?!

Jumping Around!

As You Hound

Me For Attention!

As You Pound

About In Circles!

As Every Sound

You Hear Stands Your Ear!

You Remind Me Of A Bat!

If Only You Were

Afraid Of The Light!

Knowing That

Peacefully

Serenely

Beautifully

She Sleeps

Knowing Rest

Meeting Slumber

Floating On Repose

I Suppose I

Can Only Dream Of

In Minute Instances

Of Time Immemorial

It Seems To Me

My Last Chance

Was Had To Be

Free Of Anxiety

Liberated From Fear

In Near Futures Unimaginable

By Human Standards Of Destruction

By Human Levels Of Degradation

By Human Heights Of Disillusion

Within Our Race

To The End Of A Nightmare

Life Of Unrest

Identity's Death

She Called

The Other Day

And Said

By The Way

It Was Time To Change

Her Name

It's Been The Same

As His

Too Long To Remember

How Violent His Temper

Identifies The Signature

Of Who She Was

Then

Back When

Fear Ruled Decisions

To Make Or Break

The Ties That Bind

A Mother To Her Child

For A Whiled Man

She Once Called Husband

Lover

Hovers Around Her Ear

Audible Enough To Hear

Whispers Oh So Near

To Her Mind Listening

For A Severing Of Connections

Impossible To Cut

Improbable To Gut

The Pain Away In Altered Letter

Is Better

Maybe

For All Concerned

To Spurn

Identity's Birth

No Longer

Of Any Worth

SECTION FOUR

AMERICA

Fear In San Francisco

Judge Ye Not

Lest Ye Be Judged

And Sentenced To Rot

Amid A City You've Trudged

Along Singing Your Song

Of Right And Wrong

Quoting Your Scripture

Burning The Picture

Of Compassion For All

Who Will Ultimately Fall

On Knees To Pray

On Judgement Day

Asking Forgiveness

Begging To Confess

Sins Against Our Brothers

While We Ignore The Others

Standing Always Beside

Forever To Hide

Behind A Culture

A Scavenging Vulture

Feeding On A Corpse

Of Fear

Jazz Renaissance

Ya, Man

Wish I Coulda Been There

Where The Heart O' Jazz

Began It's Beat

Pullin' The Seat

Out From Under A Blunder

Of Neat And Tidy Life

Tappin' The Feet O' Strife

Smilin' With Sweet Joy

Over That Boy

Over That Girl

In That Swirl Of Reverie

Forgettin' The Settin' Sun

Of Days

Of Years

With Tears Dried And Gone

In That Scat Song

Of Ella!
Louis!
Carmen!
Johnny!
Sara!
Sammy!

Floatin' Them Notes

Grabbin' Them Coats

And Movin' On

To The Dawn

Of The Nex' Gig

Spreadin' The Word

With Every New Blurb

Of Lyrical Magic

Happily Tragic

One In The Same

Moment Of Time

Comin' On A Rhyme

Of JAZZ RENAISSANCE!

Plea

My Freedom's Flag.
It Called To Me:

Please!
Don't Let Me Die!
I Am No Rag
To Sit Idle By
Waving Away
My Right To Fly!
Don't Let Me Die!
Please!
I Am Your Flag!
I Am Your Freedom!
I Am Your Symbol
You Say You Believe In
Me When You See
These Stars And Stripes
Risen High Upon A Pole!
I Can't Hold
On Much Longer!
You Know
Not By A Long Shot
At This Spot
Of Dog Eat Dog
Staining The Remnants
Of My Colors Bleeding
Out From A Bite Eating
Away Our Right!
To Do
For You And Me
Who Should Always Be
In Choice

In Voice

Singing Of Freedom!
To Let Me Lie
Here To Die!
Where
They Can Say
My Way
Is Cliché In This Life!
While In Truth
It Is Our Strife
To Dictate Colors
Upon Our Neighbor's House
Upon Our Neighbor's Spouse
Being Male Or Female!
Where
They Can Say
My Way
Is Cliché In This Truth!
While In Life
It Is Our Youth
To Create Terrors
Around Our Majority Opinions
Around Our Votes Against Companions
Bringing Only What
Old Age Wants!
To Kill
The Will Of The People!
Yet, Still
You Would Let Me Lie
Here To Die?!

Mourning Patrol

Morning And The Sun
Shines On His Face
Burning The Skin
Of His White Race

He Jumps In His Truck
Starts The Engine
Pets His Dog Buck
And Begins His Mission

To Weed Out All
The Immigrant Scum
Who Bring About The Fall
Of His Great Nation

Reaching The Border
He Grabs His Gun
Then Barks An Order
To His Son

Who Follows The Example
Of A Previous Generation
Filled With An Ample
Hatred For The Station
Others Can Reach
Within His Nation

Where He Will Teach
Them To Understand
That GOD Is In
His Right Hand
To Punish Sin
With Bullet And Blood

So They Can Die
Where They've Stood
Aside And Tried
To Be As Good

As He Himself
The Better Man
Might Lose His Wealth
To Those Who Can

Come And Take
Away From He

With Hoe And Rake
Ignoring Thee

Religious Right
To Hold At Bay
To Set His Sight
On Those Who Pray

For A Better Life
Within The New World
Free From Strife
Where Of This Rural
Southern Attitude
Pulls The Trigger

Upon A Mood
Of Bigoted Fervor
Hitting The Mark
Of The Poor And Lowly
Who Learn Of A Stark
Dead Centered Reality

Leaving The Body
To Rise High Above
The Dirty, The Ugly
The Hateful Unloved

That Bury The Corpse
And Keep It A Secret
Sowing No Remorse
For He To Reap It

Seeing No Recourse
To That Which Must Be Done
Killed At Its Source
Under The Burning Sun

Hot And Unforgiving
He Returns To His Truck
To Go On Living
As He Pets His Dog Buck

And Starts The Engine
Hoping Tomorrow's Luck
Brings The Last Mission
To Run Amuck
With Fearful Intimidation
To The Hateful Destruction
Of Worthless Immigration

Columbine

One Would Hope

Columbine

Taught A Lesson
Made An Impression
Offered A Revelation Of Truth
Within Our Youth Of Honesty
Among Our Ignorance Of Children
Disregarded So

By We Who Say To Know

The Story Of Columbine

Is To Learn The Lesson
It Is Teaching Of Our Sadness
Ever Reaching For An Understanding
Amid Instruction We Offer In Coffers Of Madness
Among Our Arrogance Of Self
Regarded CROW

Is This Our Flag?

This Is Our Flag.

Be Proud Of It.

Even As You Lie

Among Our Gutters Of Life

Dying From Starvation

Be Proud Of Our Nation.

Even As You Cry

Within An Empty Soul's Whole

Of Contempt For You And Your Tears

Cascading Upon The Heart Of So Named Civilization.

This Is Our Flag.

Be Proud Of It.

Book Store

There I Sat

At

The Center Of Knowledge

Reading

Understanding

Without Ever Attending College

There I Sat

At

The Center Of Facts

Studying

Contemplating

That Which Society Lacks

There I Sat

At

The Center Of Information

Figuring

Wondering

Whether Destruction Of Our Nation

Becomes Inevitable

Without Answer

For A Cancer

That Is Ignorance

Freedom's Law

One Nation

Under GOD

Separating Church And State

Contradicting Love And Hate

Continuing Opinion's Rate

Of Growth Exploding

Outward Enveloping All

Inward Who Care Not

For One Or The Other Brothers

And Sisters Aside To Ride Upon

The Coat Tail Of The Strongest

Statement Punctuated By A Gavel

Will Unravel Freedom's Law

Gay Marriage

Constitutional Amendment

Changing A Name

"FREEDOM"

Cementing A Game

"EMANCIPATION"

Contradicting A Frame

Of Our "NATION"

Misunderstanding

The Very Basis

Of Our Rationale

Built Upon All Men

Created Equally Ignorant Then

Of That Which They Would

Gladly Fight And Die For

Personal Preferential Treatment

Of Arrogant Assuming Attitude

War On Terror

Prayer
For Destruction Of Anger

Petition
For Obliteration Of Violence

Service
For Annihilation Of Hatred

Supplication
For Extermination Of Death

Can Be

Our Only Invasion
Worthy Of Justification

Amended

Support
The Federal Marriage Amendment

Support
Our Fear Of Change

Support
The Federal Marriage Amendment

Support
Our Judgement's Range

Of Righteous Feelings Uncontrolled
Of High And Mighty Flare

Where Anxious Conservative Fists Of Old
Show Exactly How Much We Care

To End GOD's Love So Often Sold
As A Platter Of Blood Soaked Fare

Might Makes Fright

Our Sin

Within

Our Fright

Comes To Fight

To Preserve Our Right

To Show Our Might

Along A Line Of Sight

For All The World To See

How We Can Make Them Free

To Be The Same As Thee

IGNORED DIVERSITY

We Want You

WE WANT YOU
Too
Fight For FREEDOM

WE WANT YOU
Too
Fight For JUSTICE

WE WANT YOU
Too
Fight For LIBERATION

Of Our Nation From DECENCY

WE WANT YOU
Too
Give Your LIFE

WE WANT YOU
Too
Give Your WIFE

WE WANT YOU
Too
Give Your CHILD

Of Wild Eyed INNOCENCE

A Chance To COMPREHEND

The End Of FORGIVENESS

WE WANT YOU
Too
Offer Your ARM

WE WANT YOU
Too
Offer Your LEG

WE WANT YOU
Too
Die For Those WHO

Send You To DANGER

Mend You When INJURED

Then Bill You For The COST

Of A Meal You EAT

As You Heal A Wound UNWANTED

By A Band Of BROTHERS

Ignored Yet FLAUNTED

By Your Government SPONSORS

As A Badge Of COURAGE

To Discourage The ENEMY

From Speaking Their MIND

As A Sign Of DISCONTENT

Spent In CRITICISM

Over The Free WORLD

Given A TRY

By ALL

Who Once CALLED

Upon LIBERTY

For Thee As NECESSARY

911

Let Us Find
Those At Fault

Let Us Find
Those To Blame

WHERE

Hateful
Malicious
Vicious Attitude
Remain The Same

As They Who Have
Always Been Seen
As Living The Dream

American Beam
With Pride As We Ride
A Wave Of Discontent
Spent In Complaint

Over Taxation
Over Education
Over Directions

Our Country Takes
As We Quickly Rake
In The Cash
We Are So Rash To Hoard

Away From The Poor!
Away From The Homeless!
Away From The Starving!

Worldwide Population
Within Our Nation
Building The Future
Congratulation

For The Conviction
Of Judgement Sake
Wherein We Make

Known To All
That We Call

To Arms Our Vengeance!
To Arms Our Gall!
To Arms Our Blood Lust!

For The Disgust Of Death
Is Upon Us!

Falling Sky

Oh, Beautiful
For Spacious Skies
Wherein The Rise
And Fall Of Nations Cries
Go Unheard

For Amber Waves
Of Grain
Do Stain The Land
With The Rain Of Infinite Tears
Left Undried

For Purple Mountains
Majesty
Stands As A Travesty
Of Rich Over Poor Suffering A Sore
Left Unhealed

Above The Fruited
Plain
Flowing Down A Drain
Of Rotting Righteous Indignation
Left Unloved

America!
America!
GOD Shed His Grace On Thee
Of Judgement Perverted
Forgiveness Averted
Vision Unseen

And Crown Thy Good
With Brotherhood
Between Divisive Races
Divisive Faces
Perpetually Unclean

From Sea To Shining Sea
From Land To Flowing Land
Of Milk And Honey
Sweetened With Blood
Salted With Bodies
Left Unburied
Is Our Harried Hatred
Of Life

Make Over

MAKE ME OVER
TO BE
THAT WHICH SOCIETY
SEES IN THEE
PERFECTION
UNBLEMISHED

MAKE ME OVER
TO BE
THAT WHICH SOCIETY
SEES IN THEE
SATISFACTION
UNTARNISHED

MAKE ME OVER
TO BE
THAT WHICH SOCIETY
SEES IN THEE
IDEALIZATION
VARNISHED
OVER SUPERFICIAL DISPOSITION

All You Know

That's The City
For You
Too
Push'em Out

That's The City
For You
Too
Force'em Off

That's The City
For You
Too
Throw'em Away
Today And Tomorrow
Ignoring Their Sorrow
Rejecting Their Pain
Once Again
To Disdain
Away Self Esteem
Away Self Sufficient
Means For A Peasant
To Be
Constantly
Imprisoned Below
A Most Powerful Toe
Stepping Upon
All You Know

Altamont Past

Power Scars

The Landscape Of A Once Pristine Dream

Power Molests

The View Of A Once Perfect Illusion

Power Defaces

The Object Of A Once Pure Fantasy

Power Wounds

The Earth Of A Once Primal Delusion

Of Grandeur Torn

Ripped Away

Is The Veil Of Beauty

Day By Day

Fair Share

Indian Gaming
Eight Billion A Year
A Small Percentage
For Lifetimes Of Fear
Brought By The White
Man And His Gun
Assuming His Right
Is To Darken A Sun
Day In The Life
Of The Warrior Red
Marked By The Blood
Of His Honored Dead
Slain On The Field
Of Battles Lost
Remain In The Heart
At So High A Cost
To Nations Forgotten
By History's Fate
Only To See
All To Late
The Ending Triumph
Of The True Original
Exploiting A Greed
Experienced In Past
Exacting Of Vengeance
Expected To Last
As Long
As The Land Is Old
As Deep

As The Pocket Is Bold
Enough To Give
Back The Power
Drunk And Deluded
With A Whiskey Sour
Poured Down The Throat
Of The Influential
Immigrant Unrealized
In The Affluent
Descendant Disguised
With The Face Of Want
Yet Recognized
By The Spirits Of Justice
The Souls Of Right
Who Cannot Be Wrong
In Winning The Fight
With Money Made
From The Man Of Fright
Begging On Wounded Knee
For More Than He Deserves

Pressing The People To See
The Height Of Reservations Nerve
In Succeeding
Where None Could
In Blossoming
Where None Should
Care
To Pay The White Man's
FAIR SHARE

Scapegoat

Serve Your Country

Give Your Time

So They May Blame You

For Military Crime

Leave Your Family

Your Home Behind

So They May Convict You

With Actions They Find

Appalling To See

Our Lies Exposed

In This Losing Face

Where Eyes So Closed

To Hypocrite's Stare

Judge The Line

Of What Is Fair

In Love And Time

Of War Committed

To Power Over The Weak

Who Follow The Order

To Find What They Seek

Within The Soul

Of A Prisoner's Rage

Captured In Battle

Thrown In A Cage

Beaten And Humiliated

With Unspoken Technique

Ignored And Refused

Justice To Wreak

Havoc Upon

Truth And Right

Abhorred By Those

Who Love To Fight

With Freedom's Knight

Blinded Too

A Country's Might

Enjoyed By Few

Who Understand

The Hand Of Hate

Crushes The Will

Of The Scapegoat State

Yesterday, Today, Tomorrow

A Few Of Our Sons
Died Yesterday.

A Few More Fathers
Die Today.

Still More Mothers
Will Die Tomorrow.

Such Is The Soldier's Sorrow.

But
For What?

So
We May Cut
One Another's Throat?

So
We May Gut
One Another's Bowels?

So
We May Forever Howl
For A Freedom To Hate
Within This State Of Anger?

Fail Safe

(A Dialogue Between Truth And Lie)

We Open Within An Auditorium Filled To Capacity. The Camera Is Focused On The Audience. As The Last Few Attendees Find Their Seats, Voices Are Heard Coming From Behind. We Then Turn Slowly To The Left, Eventually Facing The Stage, Where We Find Two Men In Residence There. One Begins To Speak Into A Single Microphone, While The Other Sits At A Small Table Adjusting The Sound.

GOVERNMENT SPEAKER: "Preemptive Strike!"

The Audience Is Silent.

SOUND MAN: "Can You Speak Into The Mike?"

GOVERNMENT SPEAKER: "What's That You Say?!"

SOUND MAN: "Can You Speak Into The Mike?"

GOVERNMENT SPEAKER: "Sorry!"

SOUND MAN: "That's Okay. You May Proceed."

GOVERNMENT SPEAKER: "Preemptive Strike!!"

The Audience Remains Silent.

SOUND MAN: "Can You Move Closer To The Mike?"

GOVERNMENT SPEAKER: "Pardon Me?!"

SOUND MAN: "Can You Move Closer To The Mike?"

GOVERNMENT SPEAKER: "Like This?!"

SOUND MAN: "Why, Yes. That's It. Try Again."

GOVERNMENT SPEAKER: "Preemptive Strike!!!"

Some, In The Audience, Appear Bored.

SOUND MAN: "Perhaps, The Sound On The Mike Is Too Low."

GOVERNMENT SPEAKER: "Excuse Me?!"

SOUND MAN: "Perhaps, The Sound On The Mike Is Too Low."

GOVERNMENT SPEAKER: "Can It Be Fixed?!"

SOUND MAN: "Well, Sure. There You Go. Now, Once More You Know, With Feeling."

GOVERNMENT SPEAKER: "Preemptive Strike!!!!"

Some, In The Audience, Begin To Talk Amongst Themselves.

SOUND MAN: "I Don't Think They're Listening, Mike."

GOVERNMENT SPEAKER: "What?!"

SOUND MAN: "I Don't Think They're Listening, Mike."

GOVERNMENT SPEAKER: "What Am I Supposed To Do, Now?!"

SOUND MAN: "Try Something Else They May Like."

GOVERNMENT SPEAKER: "I Imagine, You Have A Suggestion!"

Others, In The Audience, Begin To Leave.

SOUND MAN: "As A Matter Of Fact, I Do."

GOVERNMENT SPEAKER: "Well?!"

SOUND MAN: "Why, Don't You Try, Giving PEACE A Chance?"

GOVERNMENT SPEAKER: "You've Got To Be Joking!"

SOUND MAN: "Or, Maybe, Take A Stance On FORGIVENESS."

GOVERNMENT SPEAKER: "Are You Serious?!"

There Remains, No Reaction From The Audience, Excepting Those Who've Stopped Short In The Aisles. Where They Wait To See What Happens Next.

SOUND MAN: "DEADLY."

GOVERNMENT SPEAKER: "Okay, Fine!………. PEACE!"

We Hear The Small Beginnings Of Applause.

SOUND MAN: "I Think They Heard You That Time. Try Again."

GOVERNMENT SPEAKER: "Did They? Okay,….. FORGIVENESS!!"

We Cut To The Audience, As They Cheer, And Holler, And Call For An Encore.

GOVERNMENT SPEAKER: "FORGIVENESS!!!"

The Applause And Adulation Are Deafening, As We Cut Back To The Stage.

SOUND MAN: "That, Did It!"

GOVERNMENT SPEAKER: "But, I Don't Get It."

SOUND MAN: "Why, Its Obvious, Of Course."

GOVERNMENT SPEAKER: "Tell Me, Then."

SOUND MAN: "Well, Murder Brings Remorse, And Love Is The Source Of All Forgiveness. Therefore, Preemptive Strike Is Completely Unlike Anything They Wish To Understand As Freedom."

GOVERNMENT SPEAKER: "I Don't Know What To Say."

SOUND MAN: "Don't Worry, It's Okay. I'll Show You The Way."

THE END

Freedom Is

I Asked:
What Is Freedom?

I Was Told:
It Is Our Right.

To Have An American Dream
Taken Away
By A City Building A Freeway.

I Asked:
What Is Freedom??

I Was Told:
It Is Our Right.

To Deny An American Woman
Begging For A Dollar
After Buying Our Dog A Designer Collar.

I Asked:
What Is Freedom???

I Was Told:
It Is Our Right.

To Bare No Witness
To A Crime
Then Hate The American Man Who Does The Time.

I Asked:
What Is Freedom?!

I Was Told:
It Is Our Right.

To Dress Our American Child
Within The Garb Of The Robot
But Cry For The Freedom Of Individuality's Lot.

I Asked:
What Is Freedom?!!

I Was Told:
It Is Our Right.

To Denounce All Violence
Committed Against Our American Sons
While We Let Out A Cheer For Every War We've Won.

I Asked:
What Is Freedom?!!!

I Was Told:
It Is Our Right.

To Live Our Life
As We See Fit
In Destruction Of Freedoms Bit By Bit.

I Asked:

"WHAT IS FREEDOM?!!!!"

I Was Told:……….

Naivete'

Our National Security
Advisor Was Appalled
At Recent Photos Of Interrogation.

Our Presidential Opinion
Condemned The Inexcusable
Committed By Our Soldiers Of War.

Our Pentagon In Washington
Responded To Allegations
By Adamantly Denying Reports Of A Cover Up.

Are You?

Am I?
To Assume The Lie
Of Naivete'.

Do You?

Do I?
Accept The Why
We Don't Expect
These Things Happen Everyday.

Will You?

Will I?
Be America's Cry
To Deny That We As Well
As Any Other Country Will
Do To You
Or Anyone Else
What Ever It Takes
To Protect Our Way
Of Hypocritical Ray.

Near End

I Fly

My Country's Flag

For, I Believe

That Someday Rag

Nears Its End

Of Life Supreme

As Tears Do Send

A Lightning Beam

Of Death To Come

And Stake A Claim

To This Our Sum

Of Hated Fame

Indeed

Oh, My Country

How I Do Love Thee

With Scornful Eye

From Preaching Lie

Awake At Night

Do I

Question

Who's Direction?

Without Reflection

Can We Follow

A Hollow Heart

Of Vengeful Need

Indeed

Kingdom

Some Body Once Said
Off With His Head
Though It Be Long Ago

One May End Up Dead
To Joke Of His Head
Suggesting To Those We Know

Today If It's Said
Off With His Head
Our Dread Is The Terrorist Crow

For Burning In Red
Is America Communist Lead?
With Freedoms No Longer In Tow

PART TWO

LOOKING TO
THE HELL WITHOUT

SECTION FIVE

DO WE NOT

Do We Not

Do We Not

View Our Own Perspective

With Impunity

Do We Not

Picture Our Own Outlook

With Impudence

Do We Not

Approach Our Own Opinion

With Imprudence

Looking To The Hell Without

I Know God!

I KNOW GOD!

Will Forgive Me
Though I Have Trod
Upon His Children.

I KNOW GOD!

Will Absolve Me
Though I Have Run
Over His Son.

I KNOW GOD!

Will Pardon Me
Though I Have Flaunted Thee
Misunderstanding Of Him.

Evil

Creeping Along
He Sings His Song
Exciting A Sense
Of Destructive Pretense
Planning A Future
Of Bleeding Suture
Closing A Wound
Rotting Within
The Malicious Din
Of Words Berating
A Voice Of Inner Torment

Creeping Along
They Sing Their Song
Enticing Are They
Pulling Away
A Veil Of Peace
With Flourishing Sway
They Hold Over Thee
Curiosity Wondering
As Thy Back Is Turning
Will They Not Be Burning
In Voice Of Outer Comment
Stabbing The Heart Of Love

Little Love

Love Little Children

For All They Have
To Learn Of Judgement
For All They Are
To Be Taught Of Opinion

Love Little Children

For All They Understand
Of Instruction In Arrogance
For All They See
Of Education In Apathy

Love Little Children

For All They Absorb
In Training Through Anger
For All They Feel
In Tutoring Through Hate

Love Little Children

For All They Continue
To Teach Us
All That Could Have Been Just
As Easy For Us
To Become

Shunned

Abortion

Adoption

Strange

They Are

Ending

Within The Same

Syllable

Lost Love

RUN!

FIND YOUR LOST LOVE!

CATCH IT!

IF YOU CAN!

STAND!

AT YOUR THRESHOLD OF FEAR!

TO SEE IT REAR ITS UGLY FACE!

TO FEEL IT RACE IN YOUR DIRECTION!

FEEDING THAT SECTION!

WITHIN YOUR HEART!

SLICING APART!

TWO PIECES BEATING!

ONE AGAINST THE OTHER!

KILLING YOUR BROTHER!

Stream

Terrible Dreams

Horrible Screams

Red Hot Streams

Of Tears Seam

To Burn The Skin

To Scald The Cheek

To Blister The Lip

To Salt The Taste

For The Bitter Waste

Of Life

Freeway

Along The Freeway Skirting The Edge
I See My City Stretching Out Before Me
The Street Lights Of The Night Burn
Like The Embers Of A Smoldering Fire
Hiding Just Under The Surface Of Peace
The Facade Of Calm Ready To Burst Forth
Comes The New Day Into The Fray
Of Our Hectic Life With A Jagged Knife
Gutting The Bowels Within The Serene
Scene

Abyss

The Abyss

Of The Soul

The Ever

Deepening Hole

Has Widened

To A Void

Of Late

Destroyed

By Hate

Preference

When I Come Home

To Hide Behind My Wall

Of Wooden Soldiers

Standing Straight And Tall

I Feel Safe Knowing

They Can Stall

Unwanted Advance

By Any And All

Where I'm Alone Wanting

None To Call

Upon My Security

Preferred To Fall

Down To My Death

There I Lay Bereft

Of Any Feeling

Toward Friendship

Rhyme Devoid

Once Upon A Time

I Made A Rhyme

About A Lime

Bought For A Dime

With A Flavor Sublime

To Enjoy Sometime

Within The Future Grime

OF A WORLD DEVOID OF FRESHNESS

Insane Hope

Our Father

So Filled With Love

Sends Down Life

From Above

So We May Spill

Its Blood

Marveling At A Flood

Of Pain

Plugging The Drain

Drowning Insane

Hope For The Future

Life As A Violin

Gliding

Along The String

Is The Tear Drop

Of A Song Of Sadness

Trailing

Behind The Pain

Is The Line

Dampened With A Note Of Anguish

Falling

Over The Abyss

Is The Edge

Covered By A Missing Page In The Music Of Death

Mortality

Transparent Mortality

Translucent Reality

Obvious To The Eye

A Fog To Deny

Someday

WE ALL DIE

SECTION SIX

FATHERS AND SONS

Grounder

The Ball Rolls And Bounces

The Boy Runs And Announces

"I GOT IT!"

As He Fields A Grounder

From The Bat Of His Father

Instructing His Son

In Fun

BUT

As I Watch

That Father Catch

A Return Throw From His Boy

It Saddens Me

To See

An Old Memory

Within My Mind Upon A Sign

Posting Forbidden Disparaging Remark

Among A Stark Reality Centered

Around My Father

Who Would Rather

See His Son

OBEY

Having Fun

Unknown Fear

I Have Known
Many A Kind Of Fear
As A Child Standing
Among Violent Action

I Have Known
Many A Kind Of Fear
As A Boy Living
Among Painful Ridicule

I Have Known
Many A Kind Of Fear
As An Adult Being
Among Uncertain Anxiety

I Have Known
Many A Kind Of Fear
As A Man Existing
Among Hateful Malice

Yet, I Have Known
Nothing Comparing
To Any Before Known
As A Father Raging
Frightened Within
By My Child Aging
Blossoming Within
A Land Of Violent Action
A State Of Painful Ridicule
A Country Of Uncertain Anxiety
A World Of Hateful Malice
A Globe Of Fearful Truth

His Is His

What Is
     In A Name
          Brings The Shame
               Of The Father

Which Is
     Of A Blame
          Inside The Frame
               Of The Father

Who Is
     To Acclaim
          Amid The Game
              Of The Same
                    Father And Son

Done With Each Other

Fathers And Sons

Forget It.

Let Him Die.

I Have No More

Tears To Cry.

For Him

Or, Anyone Else.

Nor, Even Myself.

I Simply Don't

Care Anymore.

About A Sore

Which Is

The Human Male.

Frail And Small

As He Is.

Who Calls

My Name

To His Bedside.

Where He Will Only

Deride Me

For Leaving Him Lonely.

To Wallow Within

His Own Mistaken Past.

At Last

I'll Be Rid Of Him

Sighing Deeply

Dying From

A Lifted Weight

Of Old Hate

Upon My Shoulders.

Where An Old Fear

Upon My Soul

Carries The Whole

Of My Question.

Will I Not

Someday

Become Him?

Michael

Thus

His Dream Came True

For Two

Hundred Years He'd Waited

Or

So It Seemed To Him Then

Just Like That

It Was Here And

He Felt Such A Joy

Jumping As A Boy Just Received

His Favorite Toy To Play

For All Eternity Living

Prosperity Feeling

Sublimity Within

A Second Chance For Him

To Be Something More

Than A Sore

Upon His Father's Skin

Guilt

Guilt

He Feels

When Looking Back

Upon His Past

Upon His Life At Last

He Understands The Pain

Brought To His Wife

His Child In Wild Anger

In Moments Of Despair

Without Care For Anything

That Truly Mattered For Anyone

Newly Shattered By Anytime

Coolly Tattered And Torn

To Pieces Thrown Away

To Where His Heart Now Lay

Upon The Ground Sinking

Below The Mound Of Death

SECTION SEVEN

HUMAN

Awakened Lie

I Lie

Awake At Night

Within My Bed

Filled With Fright

By Things I've Done

Times I've Tried To Run

Away From Life

Away From Problematic Trial

While Seeking To Hide

What Is Truly Inside

My Soul

Playing A Fearful Role

Within This Dramatic

Whole Of Despair

Within This Suffocating

Coal Black Air

Filling The Lung

Of An Unforgiving One

Theatre

Spotlight!

Upon Man

Entering Stage Right.

The Curtain Is Closed

Colored Red As A Rose

Or Blood Behind Him.

Thus

Begins His Monologue:

"Ladies And Gentlemen!

Welcome To Our Show!

Tell Me.

How Many Of You Know

The Truth

Behind Our Domestic Violence?!

How Many Of You Have Seen

The Youth

Behind Our Screen

Of Proper Etiquette Presented

To Family And Friend?!

None?!

Well

I Am Here To Give

A Vision Complete!

For As I Live

I Want None To Repeat

So Heinous An Act

I Knew As Fact

In Everyday Life As A Child!
So
Husband Hold Close To Your Wife!
Lover Hold Dear To Your Significant Other!
It Is Time To Smother Your Mind Of Peace!
Behold!"

The Curtain Opens
Revealing An Empty Stage
With A Woman Alone
In Fear Of His Rage
Cowering In The Middle
Of This Unwritten Page
Waiting For The Man
To Leave His Right Stage.
He Arrives At Her Front
Without Saying A Word
Slapping Her Face
As Though Something Has Occurred
To Anger Him Enough
He Feels The Need
To Teach Another Lesson
She Must Learn To Heed.
Her Hand Covers Her Cheek
First Feeling The Sting Of Pain
As Her Tears Come To Quench
Thirst For Dominance Within The Brain
Of A Man Who Permits The Stain
Of Hate Upon His Heart

Coming To Enjoy The Art
A Ring Of Words Can Impart.
Upon This Reason For His Troubles
Where To The Surface Bubbles
Disdain For Woman
Her Reign Of Anguish
Forever Crying
Over Any Little Prying
Into Her Mind Of Twisted Thought
Vicious Words Have Wrought
From The Mouth Of Man
Where Madness Can Have Life
In The Beating Of His Wife.
In The Punishment Of His Love
Falling To The Ground
Seeming To Drown As Tears Surround
And Mix With Blood Dripping
From Her Lip Ripping
In Two And Three
In Four and More
Pounding Fists
Against The Face Of Woman.
Screaming In Hatred
Is She
Is He
Stopping In Motion Weaving
In Breath Heaving
Letting Go And Leaving Center Stage

Returning To The Right Of The Page.
The Curtain Is Closed
Colored Red As A Rose
And Blood Behind Him.
Thus
Begins His Lecture:

"Descry!
That Which You See Here Before Thee!
Reject!
That Which You Know As Our Sad Show!
Spurn!
That Which You Feel As A Superior Zeal!
For Now
You Must Understand!
As I Hold My Hand
High In The Air
Bloodied And Bruised!
This Has Been Excused
Too Long!
This Is Wrong!
So
Husband Go Home
Hold Close To Your Wife!
Lover Leave
Hold Dear To Your Significant Other!
Refuse To Smother
Another Mind Of Peace!"

Irony

She Screamed

As She Ran

To Where

She Dreamed

As No One Can

For There

She Beamed

Until Her Span

Of Life Would Dare

Come To An End

Suddenly, Sadly

Destroyed By Forgetting

Who She Was

Fault Line

Sadness Pervades
Upon The Face Of The Human
The Thin Red Line
Of The Mouth
Is Straight

Anguish Invades
Upon The Space Of The Human
The Thin Life Line
Of The Heart
Is Weight

Sorrow Cascades
Upon The Race Of The Human
The Thin Fault Line
Of The Mind
Is Hate

Do You See?

Do You See?

Ethnicity?

How Much Hate?

Envelops Thee?

In Colors?

Light Or Dark?

In Tones?

Smooth Or Marked?

In Hues?

Blinding Views?

You Choose To Be?

Two Parts Being

That Part Of Me.

THAT PART OF ME.

That Seeks To Destroy

My Connection With GOD

My Connection With Man

Has Surfaced Of Late

As A Handy State Of Being

ANGRY

VINDICTIVE

APATHETIC

JUDGEMENTAL

HEARTLESS

A Part Less

Of The Joy Of Happiness

Eccentric

Tell Me
Of Your Eccentric Mind.

Tell Me
Of Your Uncommon Kind.

Are We
Truly All That Different?

Can We
Be All That Immensely Reverent
Of Opposite Ends Of The Spectrum Of Life?

Surely
Not All That Completely Divergent
Of Common Strands Of The Dictum Of Strife?

So Much Nonsense

We Hear So Much

From The Mouth Of Man

That Life Is Sacred, Yet

Man In His Infinite

Superiority Murders Indiscriminately

Everyday Not In The Life

Of The Human, But In The Life

Of All Being We Continue Seeing

As Irrelevant

Surrounded

Surrounded

Hounded

Soaked

Choked

Drenched

Incensed

At A Blackness Around The Soul

Of Man As A Mole Can

Borrow For Life Underground

So Does The Whole Of Human Understanding

Dive Deeper Down To The Keeper

Of Evil Inviting All Who Will

Listen For A Call To Arms

Amid Violence So Immense

Is Our Hatred Of Love

Point

I Think
I'll Post A Reward
For The Conviction Of Animal Cruelty
For The Punishment Of The Abuser
The User Of Pain
Who Makes His Point
With Force And Fist

I Think
I'll Post A Reward
For The Acquittal Of Human Compassion
For The Forgiveness Of The Judge
The Smudge Of Stain Upon The One
The You And Me
Who See No Point
In Giving To The Living Homeless Person
The Begging Hungry People
Who From The Steeple
We Pray Too
Appear Just
As Worthy Within The Eyes
Of The Ultimate Understanding
Radiating Downward, Yet
Dissipating Outward, Set
To Die
Away As The Stray

ANIMAL WE

So Deeply Care For

Mouth

The Mouth

Of Man Can

Cut And Slice

Nice And Naughty

Haughty And Nimbly

Speak To The Meek And Lowly

With A Force Devoid Of Remorse

Over Preference For The High And Mighty

With An Awe Full Of Course

Over A Self Indulgent Arrogance

Violenceus Domesticus

How Can You
Do This Thing
Even While You
Wear The Ring
Of Love Professed
About Your Breast
Of Hearts Beating In Rhythm
Within One Another's Mistaken
Vision Of Harmony
Mocking You
Am I

For

Can I
Not Forget
Your Regret
In Ever Believing The Lie
Deceiving Your Sigh
Of Fantasy's Cry
Of Faith You Saith
Someday I Shall Find
My True Love
My Turtle Dove
Among A World Of
Empty Souls

Sensibilities

CAPABILITY

BEGETS

CULPABILITY

REGRETS

RESPONSIBILITY

FORGETS

COMPATABILITY

WITH

SENSIBILITY

Opinion

No One WANTS
To Hear It.

Everyone HAS
To Fear It.

No One WANTS
To Listen.

Everyone HAS
A Vision.

No One WANTS
To Understand.

Everyone HAS
To Hand

Down A Sentence Of JUDGEMENT
Along A Statement Of DAMNATION
Over Man And His Infinite STAND
Against Alternative VIEW
OF
WHAT IS TRUE?

Pretension

A Waterspot
Stains His Luxury Vehicle

A Footprint
Marks Her Brand New Floor

A Neighbor
Threatens Their Property Value

A Neurosis
Dirties Our Mind Numbing Phobia
For Proper Appearance Adherence To Set Criteria
Guided Along Familial Advice Thrice
Imbued And More Rude Attitude
Excepted In Light Of All Love
Lost
When Tossed Out A Window
Of Clearly Muddled Pretentious Rebuttal

Abuse

Happens Every Day

Right?

Comes With Every New Ray
Of Sunshine Blight
Darkened To A Cloud
Of Blackened Heart?

Isn't That Correct?

Tell Me.

It Isn't True?

You And I
Understand What It Is
To Cry?

You And I
Understand What It Is
To Lie?

Within A Pit
Of Anger?

Ripped Apart
By Fangs Of Violence?

Torn In Two
By Pangs Of Guilt?

To Wilt Our Flower
Of Youthful Hope
Unable To Cope
With Hate?

Childhood

Must Have Lost It
Then Again

Might Have Tossed It
Or

Misplaced It
Maybe

Erased It
From Memory Forgotten

How Rotten
Futures Can Be

Without A Little Free
Childlike Wonder

Over Youthful Exuberance
In Long Past Hope

Of Long Lost Love
Above The Mind

Below The Heart
Tearing Apart

The Whole
Of Excitement
In Life

Hunt

I Think
I'll Go A Hunting
Setting My Sight
Upon The Deer

I Think
I'll Go A Killing
Proving My Might
Day After Year

I Think
I'll Go A Shooting
Mouthing My Fright
So Very Near

I Think
I'll Go A Judging
Giving My Right
Within Your Ear

To Speak Of Sacred Life
While Feeding On Stalking Death
From The Breadth Of My Nostril
Scenting The Width Of My Hostile
Attitude Toward The Animal
Seen As Human Compassion
Unmatched Then Rationed
Unhatched Then Fashioned
Out Of The Shell
Of A Heart Of Hell

Void Of Distinction

There Can Be No Distinction

Between The Bug And Man

Between The Smug High Hand

And The Slug Who Leaves A Strand

Of Entrails Behind When Mutilated Under

Childish Disgust From Human Thunder

No Better Than The Slime Of Primordial

Ooze Upon The Sundial Of Time

Testing The Arrogance Labeling The Shoe

Crushing The Body Of All You

Consider Correct Instinct Erect

Along A Spine Of Yellow Line

Behind The Snail Of Slow Moving

Murder Proving True Is The Waist

To Know The Taste Of Bitter Righteous Opinion

Kind Of Blind

Ridiculed
With A Feeling Of Inadequacy?

Teased
By An Understanding Of Worthlessness?

Pushed
Into A Love Of Hate?

Is This Our Rate
Of Decline?

Is This Our Human Kind
Forever Blind To Acceptance?

Key

Education
Becomes A Key
To Gain A Love For Money

Education
Becomes A Road
Where We Kneel In Worship Of Code

Education
Becomes A Door
Through Which Mankind May Hoard

Education
Becomes A Way
We Must Follow Our Love To Spray

Red Blood Of Our Brothers
Upon The Wall Of All
Who Refuse To Agree
With The Knowledge That We
Are Above Their Inferiority

SECTION EIGHT

WORLD

Two Faces

Why Don't You
Come, America?!

Why Won't You
Risk Your Lives For Us?!

Why Shouldn't You
Remove Our Dictator
By The Bullet Of Your Gun
Retrain Our Military
Under A Burning Sun
Rebuild Our Schools
For Our Children To Have Some
Kind Of Education?!

Why Wouldn't You
Police Our State
Until We Can Be
Free?!

To Hate
Your Presence!
To Tire Of Our Troubles
Brought By You And Your Control!
We Were Told
Could Be Enforced!
For Our Use
To Abuse
You Out Of Fear
Over Your Power!
Now Souring Within
A Full Belly Feeding
Upon Mistrust!

Graffitti

Foul Language

DIrty WOrdy RHymes

DATes ANd TIMes

SHOWing ANd GROWing

DISGUST IN LUST

Abortion

LIFE!

Begins There
Where
Judgement Ends
Where
Opinion Sends
A Message It Is
No Longer Of Any Consequence

LIFE!

Begins There
Where
Anger Halts
Where
Hatred Salts
A Taste To Be
No More Of Any Concern

LIFE!

Begins There
Where
Violence Stops
Where
Protest Mops
Down Our Tears
No More For Anyone
Else But Ourselves
And Our View
Of All That Is True
To You Or Me
Who Cannot See
The Reality
Beyond Our Awareness

Feel

Feel

Like Crying

For The World

It Is Dying

To Write

It's Own Epitaph

To Speak

It's Own Eulogy

Dripping In Irony

Fly

My, My
What An Ugly Little Fly
You Are
Here To Annoy
Here To Toy With
My Peace
Full Of Reverie
My Calm
Filled Unexpectedly
By Your Presence
In My Wondering
How To Explain Your Existence
Within This World
Where Life Is Considered
Sacred By Most
Who Toast Their Own
High Minded Ideal
Yet Boast Of Their Own
Bloodthirsty Zeal
To Kill A Disgust
In Your Lust
For Decayed Matter
Yet Still Feel Just
In Disgust Of Abortive
Measures Defined
As Crimes Against GOD
Sins Over Trod By Man
Who Stands In A Hateful
Judgement Over
Your Broken Wingless Body

One Owner

We Own

But One Car

Yet The Scar

Of Pollution Is Upon Us

We Own

But One Vehicle

Yet The Sickle

Of Smog Bleeds Us

Of Our Rightful Heir

Apparent Is The Snare

We Set For Ourselves

Wasteland

BLOOD

Upon A Frozen Wasteland

A Metaphor For The Heart

Of A World With No Hope

Of Thaw So Raw And Seeping

With An Ooze So Cold and Creeping

Over Slowly Covering With An Icing

Over Cunningly Crushing With A Killing

All Compassion Flowing With A Waving

Away Of Light And Love

Away Too Might Our Dove

Of Peace Soon Disappear Within

This Sin This Wintry Weight

Buried Beneath A Headstone

Of Frigid Biting Death

Sap

We Cannot Sleep

Where Nightmares Creep

We Cannot Rest

Where Anxieties Test

We Cannot Nap

Where Strength Is A Sap

Oozing With A Weakness

Of Daily Hypocritical Error

Beyond

Oh
Someday
To Feel No Need
For Rest To Ponder
An Existence Beyond Comprehension

Oh
Someday
To Feel No Need
For Calm To Consider
An Occurrence Beyond Understanding

Oh
Someday
To Feel No Need
For Peace To Contemplate
A Presence Beyond Realization

Roar

Roaring Into The Future

Shouts The Wall

Of Elementary Education

Rooted In The Past

Speaks The Barrier

Of Unchanging Attitude

Truth Be Told

Step Lightly
Dancing Youth
For The Truth Of Life
Is More Dangerous
Than You Can Imagine

Step Cautiously
Prancing Child
For The Wild Winds Blow
With A Strength
You Cannot Understand

Step Warily
Jumping Maiden
For The Monsters Den
Is More Horrible
Than You Can Conceive

Tabula Rasa

Dramatic Double
Triple Timed
Classical Rhymed
Musical Wine

Presenting To The Mind A Beating
Of The Drum A Feeling
Of The Sum Of All Fear

In The Soul Of All Offering A Pounding
Of The Piano Key Drowning
In The Fists Of Fury's Kiss

Rising To A Falling From The Heart
Of The Child Dripping
With Pain Filling An Ocean

Of Tears To Rain Upon The String
Of All Violins Flooding
Killing Hopeless Dream

In The Life Of The Wife Screaming
In Anguish Crying
Inner Torment Over

A Long Lost Night In Shining
Armor Emptied Of Love

Meadow

Lush
Green Grasses
Thick And New

White
Puffs Of Cotton
Dotting A Sky Of Blue

Tall
Yellow Wildflowers
Offering Sweet Scented Views

Alas

Are Gone
In Time To Run
Away From A Spray
Of Blood Red Flowering
Towering Over Peace
Comes The Nightmare
Of The True
Specter Of Life

Ocean

Looking

Across A Blue Void

Sees Nothing Obstructing

Exposing

Loneliness Washing

Over The Side

The Barrier

Of The Raft Of Life

Leaking

Filling

With Tears Pouring

Down The Round

Curving

Surfacing Red Hot

Colors Of Anguish

Upon The Cheek

The Meek

The Lowly

Slowly Dying

A Death

From The Breadth Of Apathy

Rabbit

Please!
Be Fruitful!
Multiply!
So Much To Die!
A Death Of Overpopulation!
A Life Of Starvation!
A Breath Of Every Nation
Choking On An Heir
Of Sheer Number!
Coughing Up A Fear
Of Giving Our Living
Away To Another
Unwanted Child!

YET

Please!
Don't Stop!
Multiply!
Be Fruitful!
Grab Another Snoot Full
Of Consolation!
In The Knowledge
Of Neglection!
In The Understanding
Of Our Infection!
Spreading Our Belief
Life Is Worth
Giving A Living
Within This World
Filled To The Brim
Over Flowing In
Conceited Selfishness!

Regressive Dialogue

The City Said
To The Farm:

"Get Out Of My Way!
I Need To Stretch
My Arm."

The Farm Said
To The City:

"No!
I Do Not Think So!
You Cannot Destroy My Serenity."

The City Then
Told The Farm:

"You May As Well
Move Aside.
For, I Ride At A Fast Pace
And I Will Overtake
You Shortly."

The Farm Then
Told The City:

"What A Pity
I Feel For You.
Tell Me.
What Will You Do?
When Your People Who
Feel Their Stomach
Is Empty.
Cry Out
With Revolutionary Shout
About Mistakes
Made In The Shade
Of Progress."

Affluent Pollutant

AFFLUENCE

BREEDS

POLLUTANTS

AMONG

ARROGANCE

WITHIN

A POPULACE

TOO IGNORANT

TO UNDERSTAND

ITS FUTURE

IS AT HAND

Progress

The New

Over The Old Buried

Under Forgotten Tombstones

The Fresh

Out Of The Stale Rotting

Within Blackened Centers

Our Progress

Beginning A Regress To

Ancient Stagnant Mistake

Raking Away Nourishment's

Ill Conceived Futures

Schism

Our Want

Bringing Terror

Our Greed

Creating Violence

Our Need

For Jeweled Prism

Indeed

A Parting Schism

Pollution

Of Course

It Saddens Me

Such Beauty

Can Be

Destroyed

So Quickly

BUT

What Do You Expect?

We Are The Human Race

The Very Face Of Cancer

Spreading Our Infection

To Every Section

Of The Earth

FOR

We Will Never Be

Satisfied Until

Our Home Is Gone

Forever

Under The Weather

Of SMOG
CHEMICAL FOG
APATHY ABOUT

The Snout Of A Sow

Feeding In The Trough Of Life!

Earth Day

Happy Earth Day!

Happy Birth Day!

To A New Generation

Hoping For The Best.

At The Jest Of The Previous

Destructive Force.

Coursing Through

The Vein Of The Old

Cold Veneration Of Age.

The Bold Reverential Cage.

Locking Out The Chance To Eat

A Fresh Ideal Meal.

Musical Showcase

Children

Perform Here Before Us

Present Your Future Chorus

Of Hope For The World And Its Tune

In The Voice Of Youth And Its Note

In The String Of Growth And Its Beat

In The Drum Of Knowledge And Its Measure

In The Horn Of Joy And It's Harmony

In Tomorrow's Plan

Where Someday Stands

A Chance For All To Be

Somebody Understood By Society

Acknowledgements

No book could ever be written within the vacuum of space we create for ourselves, and for this reason I would like to acknowledge the following:

I give thanks to GOD, for without him I would have nothing.

I thank my Wife and Daughter for their unending love, patience, attentiveness, and encouragement while providing an audience for my work.

Thanks to Nona DeSantiago (MOM), for not only financial support, but for believing in me as a person no matter what I chose to do.

Thanks to Richard Foster for reading my work without being asked, and for his fresh perspective.

Thank you Kathy and Bo Tracewell for technical support.

And, I THANK YOU, the reader, for your time and attention. I truly hope your life will always be filled with love and forgiveness, given and received, by our fellow brothers and sisters.

Sincerely,

Alexander R. DeSantiago
September, 2004

About the Author

Alexander R. DeSantiago has written four volumes of poetry, of which volume four is the first to be released. He is currently working on a novel and his next collection of poems simultaneously. He lives in California with his family.

ISBN 1-41204466-9

Made in United States
Orlando, FL
26 September 2023